Atlantic Canada

Atlantic Canada

Sherman Hines

Nimbus Publishing Limited

Nimbus Publishing Limited
P.O.Box 9301, Station A,
Halifax, Nova Scotia
B3K 5N5

CANADIAN CATALOGUING IN PUBLICATION DATA
Hines, Sherman, 1941-
Atlantic Canada
ISBN 0-921054-03-3
1. Atlantic Provinces – Description and travel – Views.
I Title.

FC2004.H56 1989   971.5'04'0222   C89-098515-4
F1035.8.H56 1989

Printed and bound in Singapore
by Khai Wah Litho Pte Limited

Frontispiece: Prospect, N.S.

Right: Jerrys Nose, Nfld.

North Shore, P.E.I.

Left: Fundy National Park, N.B.

Overleaf: Fishing, Tabusintac, N.B.

Dairy farm, Rawdon Hills, N.S.

Left: Eglise Sacré-Coeur, Digby County, French Shore, N.S.

Harvesting, P.E.I.

Blue Herons, Tracadie Bay, P.E.I.

Peggys Cove, N.S.

Winter, Marshy Hope, N.S.

St. Andrews, N.B.

Right: Market Square, Saint John, N.B.

Quisibis, N.B.

Bay Bulls, Nfld.

Building up for a storm

Right: St. James Roman Catholic Church, Summerfield,P.E.I.

Jack Russell puppies, Poplar Grove, N.S.

Right: Period House, Grand Manan Island, N.B.

Overleaf: Mother and children, Poplar Grove, N.S.

Fishing village, Nfld.

Left: Anchored in the harbour, Nfld.

Coffin Island, Liverpool Bay, N.S.

Fishing fleet, Meteghan, N.S.

Grand Manan Island, N.B.

Surf, Ferryland, Nfld.

Fisheries Museum of the Atlantic, Lunenburg Waterfront, N.S.

G. L. Snow, Victoria, Conception Bay, Nfld.

Stud farm near Fredericton, N.B.

Green Gables, P.E.I.

Beaverbrook Art Gallery, Fredericton, N.B.

Lunenburg Academy, Lunenburg, N.S.

Cow Head, Nfld.

Iceberg, East Coast of Labrador, Nfld.

Overleaf: Peggys Cove, N.S.

St. John's, Nfld.

Saint John, N.B., from Market Square

Swallowtail Light, Grand Manan Island, N.B.

Lapstrake boat, Winterton, Nfld.

Minnow fishing, Robertsons Cove, N.S.

Gathering moss, North Shore, P.E.I.

Abandoned farm, Havelock, N.B.

Rowboat, Ingonish, Cape Breton, N.S.

Peggys Cove, N.S.

Lobster fleet, Rustico Bay, P.E.I.

Vernon Falls, P.E.I.

Mallard hen with ducklings, Tantramar Marsh, N.S.

Raccoon, Little Pond, P.E.I.

Lumber mill, Sherbrooke Village, N.S.

Overleaf: Tobacco crop, P.E.I.

Peggys Cove, N.S.

Right: Blue Rocks, N.S.

Floats, West Dover, N.S.

An Island farm, P.E.I.

Model-ship building, Voglers Cove, N.S.

Bluenose weather vane, World Trade and Convention
Centre, Halifax, N.S.

World Trade and Convention Centre, Halifax, N.S.

Queen St. Inn, Halifax, N.S.

Historic Properties, Halifax, N.S.

The Bluenose at her berth, Halifax Waterfront, N.S.

Overleaf, left: Mersey River, Liverpool, N.S.

Overleaf, right: Broken lobster traps, Cavendish Beach, P.E.I.

Monkstown, Nfld.

Right: Monkstown, Nfld.

Overleaf: Winterton, Nfld.

Sandy Cove, N.S.

Left: North Shore, P.E.I.

Overleaf, left: Old salt, Nfld.

Overleaf, right:Bluenose II under sail, Halifax Harbour, N.S.

Model boats, Conception Bay, Nfld.

Right: Moored, Kennebecasis River, N.B.

Standing on guard, Louisbourg, Cape Breton, N.S.

Left: Fall River, N.S.

"Swinging the cat," Mahone Bay, N.S.

Left: Throwing the hammer, Highland Games, Antigonish, N.S.

Overleaf, left: Bill DeGarth, sculptor, Peggys Cove, N.S.

Overleaf, right: Rock-strewn shore, Broad Cove, N.S.

Fishing shacks, St. Peters Harbour, P.E.I.

Left: Oil rig, Halifax Harbour, N.S.

Overleaf: Lobster traps on wharf, Peggys Cove, N.S.

Living close to the sea, North Rustico, P.E.I.

Right: Coming home from school to a traditional saltbox
house, Nfld.

Sled dog, Nain, Labrador, Nfld.

Right: Building an igloo, Nain, Labrador, Nfld.

Peggys Cove, N.S.

Peggys Cove, N.S.

Old stone house, c. 1705, Poplar Grove, N.S.

Creek in winter, near Ingonish, Cape Breton, N.S.

St. John's Harbour, Nfld.

Left: Robertsons Cove, Stonehurst, N.S.

Christ Church Cathedral, Fredericton, N.B.

Rocky Falls, New Perlican, Nfld.

North Shore, P.E.I.

Left: Power lines at sunset, Five Mile Lake, N.S.

Overleaf: Weirs, Grand Manan Island, N.B.

Coming into Halifax Harbour, N.S.

Ingonish Beach, Cape Breton, N.S.

Dory, Blue Rocks, N.S.

Right: Purdy's Wharf, Halifax Waterfront, N.S.

Vernon River, P.E.I.

Left: Dingle Tower, North West Arm, Halifax, N.S.

Kings Landing Historical Settlement, N.B.

Hay Bales, Kings Landing, N.B.

Meteghan, N.S.

Right: Acadian flag, Maximeville, P.E.I.

Indian Harbour, N.S.

Left: Berwick, N.S.

Fisherman's dock, Nfld.

Left: Weatherworn fisherman, Nfld.

Overleaf: St. Peters Harbour, P.E.I.

Medway River, Mill Village, N.S.

Right: Sloops, Digby, N.S.

Tide line, N.B. coast, Grand Manan Island, N.B.

Left: Weir fishing, Grand Manan Island, N.B.

North Cape Light, P.E.I.

Left: Stanhope Beach, P.E.I.

Sunset, Peggys Cove, N.S.

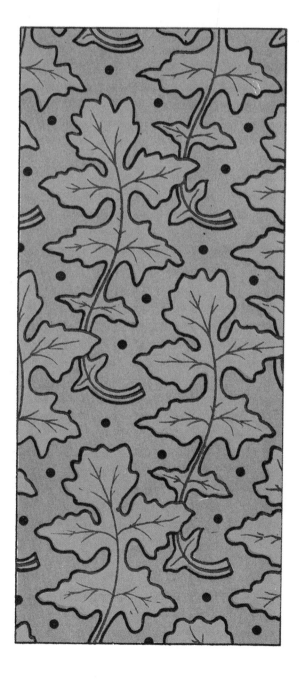

4

5

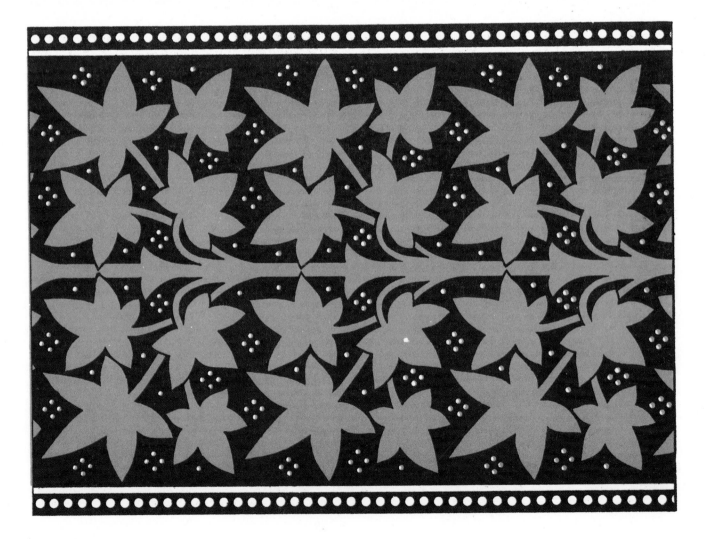

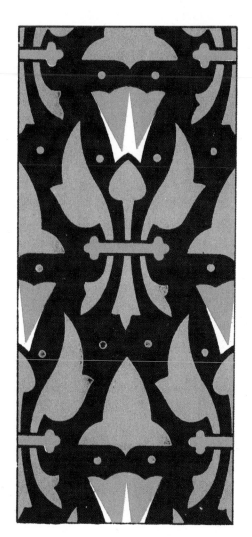

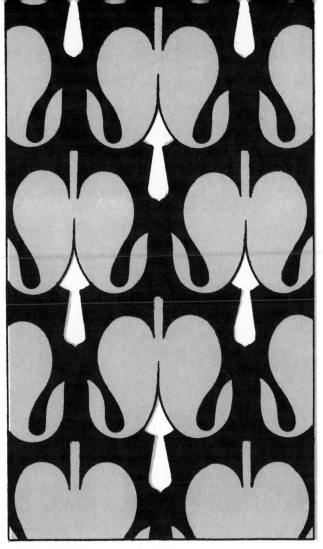

9

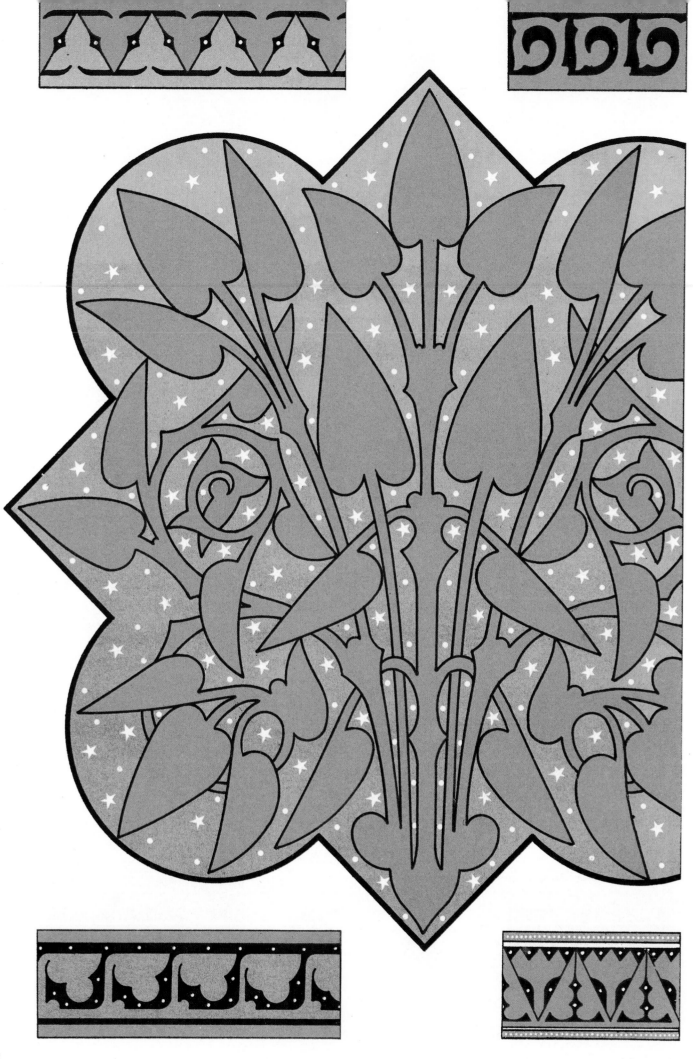

10

12

13

15

16

17

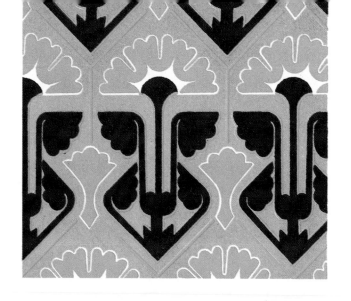

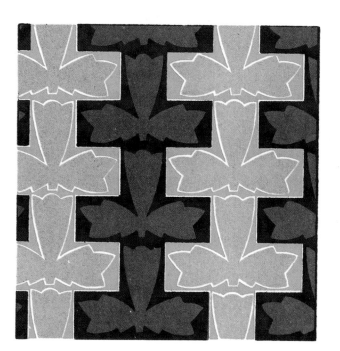

19

23

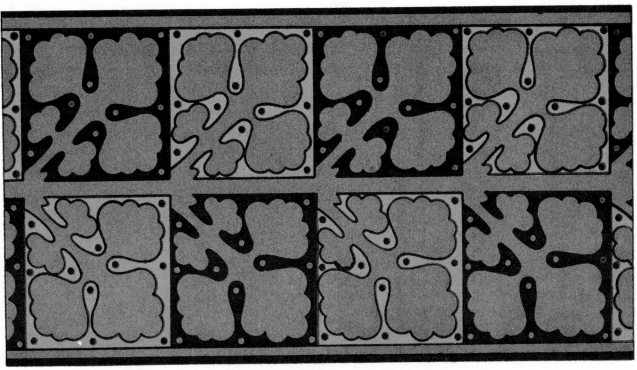

24

25

26

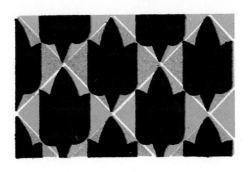

28

29

30

31

32

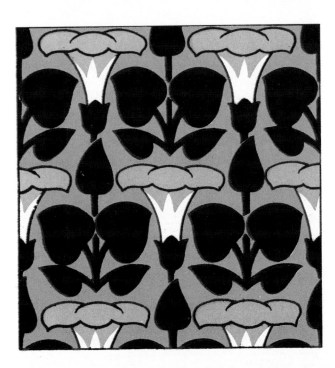

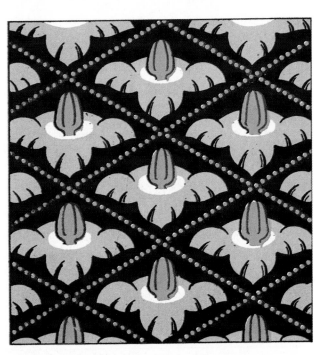

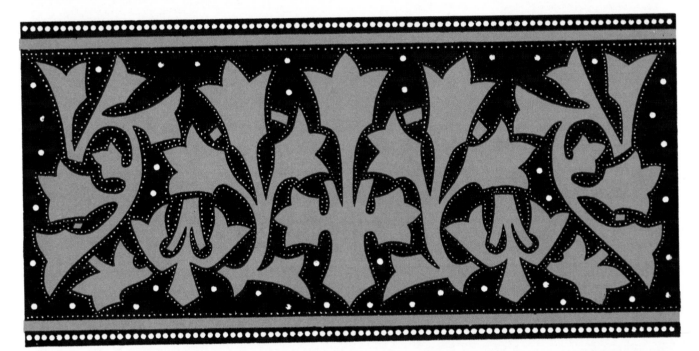

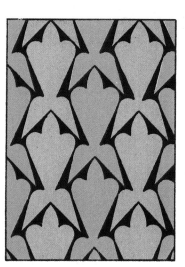

37

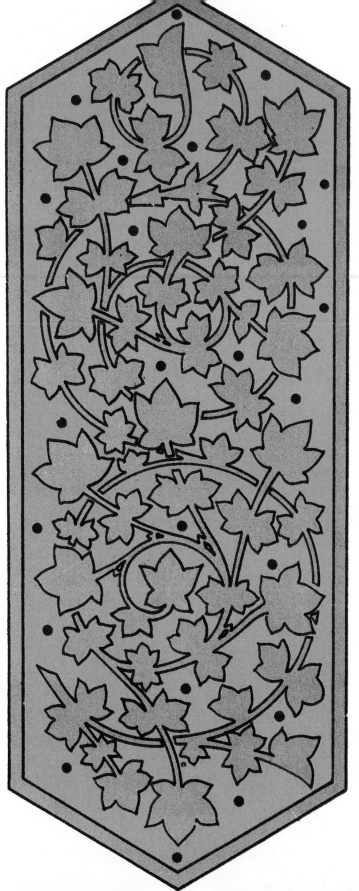

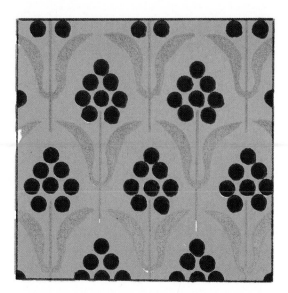

39

40

42

Original chromolithographic title page and colophon.

THE END

SUGGESTIONS IN FLORAL DESIGN BY F. EDWARD HULME F.L.S.

CASSELL · PETTER & GALPIN
LONDON · PARIS · & NEW YORK.